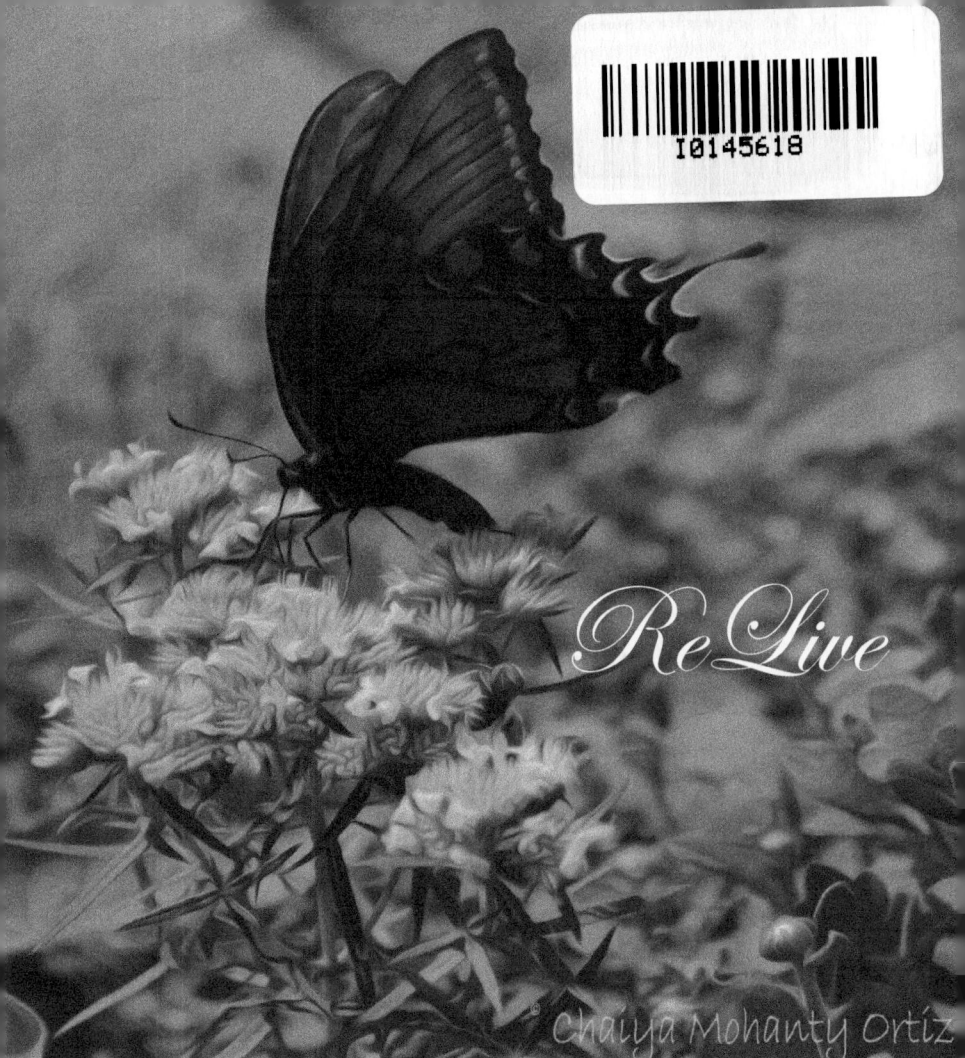

ReLive

Chaiya Mohanty Ortiz

Chalet A. Jean-Baptiste

WRITTEN IN THE SPIRIT LLC

Chalet Jean-Baptiste/Written in the Spirit LLC
Gainesville, Virginia 20155
www.chaletswits.com

Publisher's Note: This is a work of fiction. Names, characters, places, and incidents are a product of the author's imagination. Locales and public names are sometimes used for atmospheric purposes. Any resemblance to actual people, living or dead, or to businesses, companies, events, institutions, or locales is completely coincidental.

Book Layout © 2017 BookDesignTemplates.com

ReLive. Chalet A. Baptiste -- 1st ed.
ISBN 978-1-7327031-0-0

This book is dedicated
to the most powerful woman I know, my grandma,
Virginia Harvey,
who turned tragedy into triumph
and came from nothing, to give us everything.

When life breaks you and carries your spirit with it, go on a journey within yourself to find YOU again. And, with an inner death, lives another chance to try again, breathe again, revive your spirit, renew your mind and heart, and live again.

Chalet

The Death ....page 13

The Process ....page 50

The Awakening ....page 92

Preface

ReLive was born from an unconscious death that took place inside of me.

In 2006, my future husband and I and our two children left New York City and moved to Dallas, Texas in hopes of a new start at life. My life in NYC had been great. I was making six figures working as a writer for a respectable financial firm and I was teaching college English at night. I had my own two-bedroom apartment, drove a year-old Lexus, my mother and grandmother lived on the same block, and I had fallen madly in love with a man with whom I went to high school. Almost a year earlier, I had given birth to his son and he accepted and treated my daughter as his own.

After attending a T.D. Jakes Manhood conference and discovering some friends who lived in Dallas, my boyfriend suggested the move. Secretly, I was trying to break free from the emotional hold and control my mother had on me. Living down the block, she was privy to all of my affairs and always made her opinion known, even by force. So when I found out that I was not the only apple in my boyfriend's eye, I felt the change could jumpstart our family. I will never forget the exhausting 26-hour drive from Brooklyn, NY to Hurst, TX. My boyfriend had been offered a job, and so had I, teaching at a high school in Oak Cliff in Dallas, and college English at a local community college.

A year later, we were married.

We moved at least ten times in Texas, followed by a move to Virginia Beach, VA., and then finally to Manassas, VA. In 2013, my husband and I separated. I WAS FINANCIALLY, EMOTIONALLY, AND SPIRITUALLY BANKRUPT. My husband was a serial monogamous who had escaped multiple pregnancies by various women. The worst part was that I knew and accepted it for many years, all in the name of love. After two miscarriages, we had a daughter, Elise, who was born in 2012.

Although I loved Elise, something in me was broken. I had been fighting for my marriage for so long that I could no longer write or laugh or participate in LIFE. I was depressed and my bedroom became my sanctuary. My children and the little things that used to bring me so much pleasure didn't bring me any joy. My oldest daughter was disappointed, as she witnessed the outbursts and the horror story that I had become. I had relinquished my strength for a man.

When I looked in the mirror, I didn't know who was staring back at me. When was the last time I danced around the house listening to music? When was the last time I did anything by myself, for myself? Even in the last years before my separation, I was lonely. I had to beg my husband for dates and quality time. When the money wasn't right, it was because of the money; and, when it was, he didn't come home. He said I didn't cook or clean enough, even when I worked two jobs and he kept losing his. I thought I wasn't pretty enough because he preferred Latina and European woman; my black wasn't beautiful.

The first year of the separation was confusing. How did I lose this fight? How am I now a single mother of three children? How am I going to make it alone? Why does our son keep crying and asking for his daddy? I was a fixer, yet I could not fix this. I was a fighter, yet this was a battle too big for me. No matter where I'd run, I'd come back to the same type of man I was trying to escape. Of course, there was God, but I felt He had forsaken me. He had ignored my tears. He had turned a blind eye to my suffering.
Then, one day sitting on my bed, reflecting on my life, I died.

It was September 11th, 2015. I had just been released from the jail, facing a felony charge for biting my husband in a bitter fight after catching him in a hotel room with another woman. A month earlier, I was carrying our fourth child. I was now feeling like I was going to lose it all—a feeling I spared my husband from feeling many times.

Of all the fights and moments that I could have pursued his aggression towards me, he never faced a felony charge and I always dropped the charges, even hiring a lawyer on his behalf. I looked at my children and the lie my life had become and wondered where it all went wrong. There had been deaths that had taken place in me for years and the bodies were beginning to smell.

But, when I awoke, I began to put back the pieces. I had forgotten the NYC girl who defied odds – born as a "miracle" child, raped at 13, and escaping death many times. I realized that I was not just suffering from a broken marriage, but from wounds that started in my childhood. And although I could dress up the outside, with my great career and personality, inside I was still hurting. My fight had died and I had relinquished my power to those who never deserved it. I was suffering from silent depression, writer's block, low self-esteem and worth. I had married a man who represented the girl I used to be and, in saving him, I thought I was saving the little girl in me too.

In discovering this death, I began searching for life. In this new life, I defined my identity, my worth, my ability…that my black is beautiful, no matter who doesn't see it. I discovered that I was born with purpose and destiny. I began reaffirming who I am and praying 6am every morning (with the help of my mom). And, I began thanking God for what I have—my parents, my grandma, my children, my life, and my friends. And, I see things that's not, as though they are. It's a process, and God is not through with me yet. The hand of God has always been on me.

No longer will I accept going through life's motions, like a zombie searching for the first sight of life. I choose not only to survive, but live. When life knocks you down, out, and over; and you've given up and death has crept into your spirit—roll over, get back up, and RELIVE!!

Chalet

The Death

905

We stayed in 905 in that southern state
I didn't want to look at you
because the truth was
I was broken and couldn't breathe
I was thinking my beauty had disappeared
and the only thing that had life were my tears
that were all dried up

I hadn't gotten on a plane for years
I forgot how it felt to fly

I thought that maybe I'd stay there
in the air and never touch
ground again because life
on earth had turned
over too many times for me
and dropped me off in hell

But you reminded me
of my youth when I
was desired and we
loved for free

just because we could
just because we knew how
Adele's song, "When we were young,"
played in my head and we
laughed about our happy
and sad moments of 13, 14,
15, 16, and so on before
life started to move too fast
then fade
before things became
so serious- then wrong

I didn't want you to see that something
happened to me and I missed
the hero inside of you who loved me
in spite of
you always picked me up even when
you didn't know where I had been

And when we touched
I thought I saw our skin blend
so, I quickly pulled away
because your chocolate is deeper
and I didn't want to lose my complex-ion

When we made love
I didn't want to confuse
the moment that was either
two broken souls needing release
or wondering what could have been
if I wasn't so stupid to think
there was better out there

Around 9:05, we were revived
singing to music from our
younger years thinking of the loves
who left us scarred
escaping to places where others
had been for the same reasons

But I wanted to stay in the minute
the hour and dance
totally lose control
but I thought
I cut all my hair off, I wouldn't look the same
And I was thinking so much
I'd be faking the freedom

I wanted to feel again, but I didn't know

how to start again
then you looked at me

you made me feel
I was 16 and Fresh and I thought about
the power we could be
together
If it wasn't too late
If it wasn't too soon

Those two days gave
me back so many years

When we hugged
I didn't want to let go
or say goodbye
I wanted to stay there
and cry, and let it all go
to your, "It's Ok"
instead, my pride stopped me
I heard you say it anyway
in those two days
where I brought the winter with me
in a sunny state

in 905

The History of Us

I was standing in-between
it all like a hologram
looking at both sides
trying to decide
between my heart and my mind

When I was about to choose the heart
I saw him standing there
towering over me
leaning like the Eiffel Tower
wavering, as the wind blew
and waves crashed running
hitherto another, another
anything, but me

The mind spoke another truth
That I had accomplished all except him
he was the battle that I could not win
all my degrees and wit
could not satisfy his beast within
and my children became memories
of him

Who had I become in this decade
of chasing him?
boldly broken polished,
yet unrefined
searching
for what I had too easily
given away like I was on
a "Clearance" rack or
"For Sale" sign

My parents wondered what was
part of me that accepted so little
allowed me to be treated so low
when all I wanted to do was
to let it ALL GO

All the women who I thought
were prettier because
he had captured photos
in the midst of the pity party
I threw for myself because
my hair was fickle at its best
I carried and wore the remnants

of pain from the years of misuse
while they experienced what
made me fall in love

Or the children I lost
trying to give him one more
in a horrible manner
while he pretended it was all fine
because he had made it so
and I was merely surviving
internally dying

A thousand and one times
I waited on him to
see me
unBreak me
a thousand and one times
I prayed for God to restore
the spirit that he snatched away

I could not write anymore
about the people and places
and things
because I could not

see my reflection

All I could see was him laughing
like he had conquered a hero
dethroned a powerful queen
won a great war
with his flag in my back
to mark the victory
trampled on a soul influx
disrupted a beautiful life
interrupted a woman

<u>Be</u>

He said I needed to wash
it all out
but even I knew
there were some moments
that were not safe from douche

He had left his scent on me
it could not be washed away

I was his New York girl
years too late

He was a Caribbean King
who was a dollar short
a moment too soon

Together
we were enough to see
we were to defy time, reason
and just be

The Men

The interesting ones
are the ones that
remain in memory
not the ones with normal lives
but the ones who
courageously with bravado
entered the forest
discovered new rivers
unaware of the creatures that previously
inhabited the territory

The ones who shocked us
by performing electroshock therapy
and made our tears
seem like they were laughing
back at us
those moments when he was
the center of our pain

Or the ones who spit in our souls
then smeared it onto our body parts
the most delicate skill and art of lovemaking

even when we realized it wasn't love

The men who taught us
to scream like banshees
when the spirit was about to die
or the ones who revived it
with little words- all deed
the ones who captured the mind
because they understood
the dysfunctions of the heart

Or the ones who lost their mind
through life's tests and trials
gave us reason to try
and try
and try until
we realized practice
doesn't make perfect
we, instead, were left
in a state of temporary insanity
until we could find
ourselves again

The men in our minds

are the ones who defied normality
or introduced us to new worlds
with movements from the moments
the ones who slipped into memory
because of time spent
searching for what we'd later learn
to hold for ourselves

Man Broken

I have seen a man
broken
by a woman
like leaves that fall off a tree and crumble
like the sun that wilts nature
like flowers that can never be replanted
like screaming "Stand"
and him unable to move or crawl
to his next space or place
like the clock that stops ticking
the computer whose hard drive has a virus
the way she stripped him of his pride
and robbed his man
and his hood
dried his tears
to make him think
he was unable to feel
or Reach
the wind that wiped off his fingerprints

I have seen a man broken
by the lady who was a tramp

and trampled all over his soul
stole his dignity
gave it to another man
she thought was more worthy

I watched her transfer
her emptiness to him
like it was permanent resting place
like it was all in the design
like he was the creator
of something and nothing
all at the same time
and suck out his dreams
spit them on the ground
then have the dogs shit on it
while she leaves him searching
searching
searching
for his spirituality
for the God who created Adam
but lost it all because of Eve

Country Girl

I was never meant to be a country girl
never meant to be one with nature
or dance with deers
or tip the cows
never meant to know all my neighbors
and marry someone from high school

But I broke all my rules when I met you
because I thought that Texas
would bring us peace
God would meet us there
everyone believed
neighbors would become our second family
but only a part of that was true

You sucked me dry
I couldn't run anywhere
but to the woods
and wolves
while you became more beautiful
more refined

I forgot how to write poetry
put on makeup
I went into the wilderness
crazy
having lost my way
screaming for help

But there was no one there
too little
everyone always wanted to pray
give it to a God
I could no longer feel
I cried
went to church more
pulled at my hair
before it started to fall out

I looked for you through the trees
became silent
when our kids questioned
"Where is he?"
"Where are you?"
I got lost in the highways
overpasses

that seemed to take me back to hell again
country fairs, revivals, strange accents

I tried escaping to those northern city lights
where I could have conversations again
play street ball
debate with people who weren't so holy
Christian
where I could feel hope again in the eyes of my people
see my beauty in catcalls
where I didn't have to wonder
If you slept with her
making a fool out of me
in a small town
in the country

You sucked woman out of me
brought me back to my girlish days
when I wasn't aware that God could make a way
when I was traumatized by my past
moving along so slow
yet too fast
to pass the days and moments
marked by pain

when I was trying to forget
life had gotten the best of me
when I wasn't the victor
tired of the fight

They laughed at me
called me "weird"
because of whatever you had told them
my hair wasn't straight enough
I wasn't light enough
our children didn't give me enough hips
I pretended
had "Come to Jesus" meetings with myself
porcelain smiles
for those times
You almost succeeded in taking the city out of me
try to transform me into
your country girl

The Some/Sum of Us

Sometimes
I wanted him
to just say "Good Morning"
but he always said something else

The days I managed to find my self-esteem
I got dolled up to hear him say
"You're Beautiful."
even when he did, his words
were followed by something else

I waited
for the "best time I ever had" with him,
but he'd always end up doing something else
after a month of being drama-free
I'd get excited that he had finally found
monogamy
and then,
I would find out there was someone else

There were nights I cried alone
knowing that he could make it right

his mind was on something else

I waited for the special days
Anniversary, birthdays, Valentine's
Days just for us
but they were always given away to everyone else

And that became the sum of us
All somes
never All

When He Left

When he left
He left behind
his fear to commit
in our short moment
I shared the things
that took others years
I introduced him
to desert places
exposed secrets
of my intimacy
and I was left ashamed
rejected
unable to see clearly because
we both got pink eye
in the same eye

And I hadn't fallen in love
but I didn't want to stop
experiencing him
or the calm
he brought into my life
or the way

he made me feel
as if he were the defender
of my emotions
the guard of my heart

I hated the signs he'd left behind
the songs we loved
the cereal we ate
the names we gave
everything I associated
with "US" because
I thought his love was real

When he left
I felt naïve that what we did
was make love and not sex
because if we had
he would have felt mine
and his would have been
too strong to walk away

We didn't have to touch
for me to feel our intimacy
even over a cup of Russian Tea

I felt connected to him
he called us "soul mates"
then, conveniently,
dropped my soul

He left me unable to settle
unable to be satisfied
with the little things
unable to commit to the big things

Fuck... I forgot

Fuck
I just realized
you ain't shit

Maybe it took too long
I had your children
let you re-name me
slave woman
for the slave that lived
inside of you, so
everything started to fall
and fade
and I forgot

That I took you
out of the projects
and your mama's home
with no job
not a penny to your name
because I thought
 you were some kind of
Mandingo King

Maybe it was the jokes you told
or the love we made
or the charm
that lied through
those pretty white teeth
that always needed fixing
that made me forget
The pills I took
because of your many indiscretions
lack of conscience
made my hair and head fall
or mind feel like it was floating away

Fuck
Where did the years go?

I want my love back
I want to get paid
for the abuse
for the loyalty that amounted
to zero to you
I just let you get away
get away with it all

run away with my spirit
throw me around like a ragdoll
pick apart the parts
you wanted to keep

Fuck…

I am in recovery
rehab
there are still parts of me I can't seem to recapture
or remember
or reverse
parts too hard
to relive
or remake

This fantasy
I made up has become
the horror story that awakes
me from my peace
robs one of her senses
Reshape the essence
of one's belief
that love is not

love at all
even after time and dedication
hope and
prayers

That love is….
What the fuck is it?
I forgot

Fucks

Momma Pat said I was badddd
like I possessed the magic
when I was broken
and I didn't know what the fuck
she was talking about
my breasts were as big
as my mouth
my stomach had an overcast
of the childbearing
of children and men

My girlfriend said she couldn't
wait until
I said Fuck you
and not Fuck you…
are you going to fuck me now?

When I finally said Fuck.... you....
Somewhere in between...
I found me
stuck between that Fuck
and the life I called you

The way you forgot
to say Fuck me
but fucked me over instead
left like I never existed
like we never existed
like our fucks didn't
amount to shit

And what birthed from it
was too easy to walk away from
and start anew saying
Fuck me
Leaving me screaming
"Fuck you"

There were times
I'd beg you
to make love to me
you said the love was made
and what was created from it
wasn't enough to recreate love again
So, you stayed fucking me
when I wanted to re-make love

like it was something that could be possessed
like the wind had not carried
it with my scent
like fucks expired with time
the way our love had

Black Women, Black Men Extinct

They demoralize us
for our kinky hair
but copy our buttocks
and lips
and hips
then are praised for a "beauty"
not innately or culturally theirs
because they "wear" it
makes it "Right"

All those housewives almost look alike
with their store bought hair
and bodies
and light eyes
because the stars don't like
the "real" Black thing
with natural hair
and real beginnings
their wealth had to reflect their wife
who is light or white
and that is "Right"

Us, sistahs, with deep degrees
powerful minds
berry that's darker than our skin
overlooked by our kind
or too into our careers
to make a proper wife
casted as "sellouts"
unfortunately, some of us are
selling our souls for a degree
or position and title
forgetting our mother tongue
our motherland
our mothers
who still live in the ghettos
and are proud
of what we have become
while we are embarrassed by them
the others of us
stay true to both of our divided selves
lose too much for it

In schools and higher education
they are teaching our history
adding their twists

they fight for diversity and inclusion
more than us because we are focused
on "Why Johnny Can't Read"
then deny us tenure
give us seven years for empirical pressures
to "save our children"
while we lose ourselves to a system
that celebrates our vast history in the shortest month
of a people who made America great
by carrying them on the backs
of our ancestors and, Mary Sue is
"teacher of the year" for teaching
our literature and famous movies
praised for other races who rescue
our kids
while we are frustrated
with no resources
no support
no recognition
no solution to an epidemic
socially, culturally, and geographically
constructed and designed
for us to fail

We are dealing with men who
hate their skin saying
international women are better
more submissive
'cause a sistah got too much mouth
or attitude
or kids
all left behind by a brother who
couldn't conceive another generation
a legacy that belonged to him
he couldn't see beyond
his own self

The prisons wait for the majority
made up of our minority
for free labor
for another broken home
refusing to rehabilitate
the mind, body, or soul
before the streets claim his spirit
or some crooked or scared
police officer claims his soul
our brothers are taught
they must always wear a guard

on their hearts
stay hard and strong
to survive
they must resist fear
even for their own sons
forgetting their needed hugs
and daddies
and daily affirmations and prayers
that secure the soul

There are so many men
wanting the Black family extinct
there are so many men
wanting the Black man extinct
there are so many men
wanting the Black woman extinct

to kill the spirit
unable to cope
refusing to live

The

Process

Karma

I was angry
seething from the pain
lost in rain
moody from the life
I thought that was
really wasn't

You put me back
out there to be amongst
the lions and wolves
unprepared
still searching for what
had been lost in you
5, 10, 11, 12, 13 years....
they all celebrated
on the Book displaying
happy faces and story book lies
and I almost became bitter
about the pictures that never
told the full story
of a world unraveling
esteem lost and of children

almost destroyed by the screams
inside of a woman who died
without leaving earth

I felt betrayed
although my career was on the rise
life seemed to restart
I had finally bought the house
I wanted for us
many years ago
when you weren't focused
on family and future

You had done the thing
you promised to never do
committed your father
and grandfather's cardinal sin
the pastor said that I had to forgive
I say that's the problem
with those who belong to Christ
they forgive too soon
forget to be mad about first
then suffer in silence

I wanted to tell the world

what you did to me

how I watched you

reach in and pierce the skin

to penetrate the heart

before you gave it a pink slip

without notice

how I was left with my face

on the front page news

looking like the perpetrator

of a love gone wrong

in a life of over a decade

of covering up your crimes

Then I heard God speak

life

real love

better days

so, I had to find myself

again

I had to love myself

again

When I did

I was able to laugh with him
in the Brownsville Pink Houses
where he lives with his mother
in her apartment, where she
welcomed his long-term mistress
with a new baby
and we joked about the creeping
and lying I had managed to escape
the minds and bodies of women he could still control

Regretfully, the pain in his eyes
lasted only a second
emptiness only a minute before
he had covered it up with his charm
I was chasing "Fool's Gold"
and he was stuck
where he had to start over
in the same place it all began

An Old Love in a Fragile Space

Maybe I thought when I saw him again, it would be like "Love Jones" or "Love and Basketball"—those black love stories that have seemed more than fairytales. Maybe everything would fall into place. I knew it was a dangerous move—reaching out to an old love that was so strong. Since he was Lauryn Hill's "Sweetest Thing I've Ever Known" and I had given him Chrisette Michele's "Best of Me," I wasn't wrong about the electric feeling and instant connection that still existed.

After seeing him, I was able to write again. I knew then that he was still a fixture of my heart—still stuck in my soul. Our worlds were so different now—a thousand miles away, restoring and figuring out if our loves were really real or forever, children attached to our situations, with pasts unresolved. There was so much that made "us" so unattainable.

I professed to wanting his friendship, but I privately confessed on wanting so much more—like that love that can't be contained or bottled. I wanted that feeling that I had when we were young and dumb and madly in love. I wanted to be touched by him to make complicated situations into what was right. I wanted to prove that time had changed and molded me into a better woman, who thinks first. My qualities were rare—morally impeccable, and I was finally healed from the drama—everything except him. I was no longer Nelly Furtado's "Like a Bird."

How would we begin? I told everyone that we'd come back together when the kids were grown to try again. But, that was so unfair to both of us. I could feel us both slipping out of control—something we couldn't afford to lose, now that our 20's had passed.

I hadn't experienced anyone but my husband since the day I met him, but his infidelities were pushing me to the edge of my conscience. And, I wanted to experience another's touch that melted in my flesh.

I wanted something that would make me forget what childbearing does to the body and mind, and the inner death my marriage brought. To feel like the 16-year-old he met years ago who was fearless and flawless and "woman hear me roar," until life showed me colors that bled off the page.

Whether something sweet or nothing came out of our meeting, I was sick over it. I sobbed that night like it was yesterday when we said goodbye, even though it was six years ago.

The Interruption

He had managed to make me feel rejected and embraced. Where, how, and when had he appeared. How did he manage to make me feel again?

I wanted to go back to the simplicity of dating the shallow guys, who made me laugh at the hollowness of their heart. I wanted to dissect their empty conversations and eat it for dinner.

Then, he came... with noble intentions, and it was like we had known each other before, in every way. He made me question my motives and want to love again. I was not comfortable with his words that pricked me and evoked thought. After a year of celibacy, he made me feel like my quest for wholeness was not good enough. My fear of falling had exposed the weakness he could break down like a hearty meal.

Was he giving me back pieces of myself? Was I the player in his game? Did he want me to fall so he could laugh like the Joker?

God and I had always had a serious, emotional relationship. Now, I was thinking that God had a sense of humor. Did I forget that the Almighty was capable of anything and I could only control those things humanly possible?

I did not answer or want to answer his calls anymore because I didn't want to answer anymore of his questions. How did the tables turn on me? Everything was almost perfect before he re-appeared. I, dedicated mom, soon-to-be ex-wife, lived above the fray... survived the pain, experienced the drama, and made final decisions. I was going to live my life giving away my heart to all worthy—except a man. Jesus Christ would become my "new man," and man's commonality would serve as a source of pure entertainment and tools for writing.

He angered me. I could not fully understand why, except that he took away my desire to date. I no longer yearned to be touched. Everything and everyone bored me. I wanted to know and see more now. I wanted to be everywhere but in his presence.

I excused my behavior by telling myself that his arms weren't strong enough, his words not definite enough, and his intentions were opposite of mine. Did he desire to suck the blood from my hands? Was I another subject for his therapeutic study? Did he want to see how far and fast I could run in the chase? Or did I fascinate him?

I had not realized, since my husband's adulterous escapades, that control had escaped me. That all games are not meant to be won and chess games sometimes ends in a draw. Spoiled by my choices and the favor that God had given me, I didn't see my tears running dry and my heart cold and abandoned from abuse.

I did not want to see that my worth had not yet equaled the total sum and my potential was lost in the dust that failed to settle. I did not want to admit that my superiority had not been fully challenged. Maybe I was totally untapped. When I looked up, I did not recognize who stared back at me. Had I given away so much that I stopped or forgot how to experience the best? Had life been so hurtful and hard that promises began to look like dreams? Love like pain?

Suddenly, I wanted to be naked, capable of crying and screaming and loving, all at the same time. I wanted to experience joy without compromise, and love without interruption.

Insecurities

We don't kiss
it's something I never liked
before I met you
now, it makes us feel passionless

this friendship is fucking me over
the way I pretend to give a fuck
about the women before me
the ones you've loved
bodies you like
sexual intensity you've shared

I have stories too
of all night longs
men so fine
but I can only contemplate you
when we are together

I watch you focus on everything else
except me
your world so full
mine over flowing with pieces

that may never fit

You never read my piece
I am squeezing in between moments
comfortably in your world
even though I am uncomfortable at times
full of fear
just to be close to you

I am looking at myself
in the mirror
wishing my butt was bigger
for the black man
I love
not pleased about the scars
bulges that I can't hide

I can compensate
other places
other ways
I don't want to
I want to feel your desire
but all I hear is why you can't right now

shit, you ain't the only one that's been broken
here I go jumping out the window for you
falling on your excuses
I got some damn good excuses
why I should have never stopped to
discover you
I don't need any more of your appreciation
no, fuck that
thank yous come too easy
I need every bit of your love

I can't tell you how many moments you've
confused me
taken me back to
my own search for internal freedom
you know how to keep me in my place
with those damn goodbye hugs

I know it's intentional
to make every minute count
I love me
You love you
so we both have love to give
you say timing is everything

I think it's overrated
so many wishing they would have done
more
with the time they had

my wish is in the knowing
if you watch me when I sleep
or let your thoughts wonder off into the moon
thinking bout me
watch me walk across a room?
or laugh at my quirkiness?
all the things lovers do
when they realize they've lost a little
control

Instead
I'm staring in the mirror
redefining myself
stopping myself from asking all those silly questions
checking out my ingredients
giving and loving too much
overextending
attached
like my mother

over analyzing and thinking too much
distant
detached
like my father
silently insecure
about us

Ode to Single Mother

I see you
I live with you
hiding in the closets and bathrooms
for temporary silence
searching for peace in the darkness
crying in the car
when the days are too long
juggling the appointments
and schedules
afraid of sickness and disease
and cars breaking down
or short school days
trying to find the balance between responsibility
and self
giving your all to what now seems to only belong to you
cherishing pieces of joy and pain
like they were married
dedicating yourself to causes
moments that run away with time to
steal your youth
disfigure the body
prearrange the mind

rob us of spontaneity and adventure
make us say "No" too much
becoming riskless on earth
but fearless for our children

Ode to Colorful Women

There are so many women
sharing their lives
with me
and others
making me stronger
I'm ashamed of the moments in my youth
when I thought that only men were needed

I am reminded
of powerful women
who took me hanging from a limb
on the other side of the tracks
running into brick walls
with eyes open
taught me how to breathe

Black women
becoming second and third mothers
made sure I didn't
fall into the dark hole
crippled
always able to reach the light

but, I cannot deny the others

Alice, my Jewish boss,
gave me an opportunity in corporate America
later, when I had learned more
grown
moved on
invited me to her son's bar mitzvah

Najat, my Middle Eastern, neighbor
picked mint leaves out her garden for my tea
made me the most delicious coffee in her home
where we'd discuss her love and sacrifice
for her family
her love for Allah
I tried to remind her that she had all she needed
for her own garden

In Texas, Lisette, Native American and Mexican heritage,
told me about her revolutionary origins
could of talked about me when my esteem
breasts hung low
took me bra shopping instead
reminded me of my worth

later, reminded me of her warrior beginnings
when she fought cancer
and won

Lisa, Black and Pakistani soul sister
since fifteen
became her own woman
so young
too early
missing high school prom
life already beginning
surviving anything thrown her way
proud of her sexuality
culture
struggle

Laura, Italian woman
who loves literature
says its "sexy"
not afraid to live
identified by her father
at an early age
as strong and outspoken
lived up her character

and made him proud enough
to cheer her on
when she graduated from college
now she's cheering me on
in the moments that matter the most
spreading joy to others
regardless of demographics or reason

Chaiya, the Indian encourager
giving gifts
her love
time and energy
for nothing at all
to the detriment of herself
but refusing to give up
let life drown her
because there's beauty
in the art of it all

Then, there was a time
I was escaping
still unable to move
going nowhere
but everywhere fast

travelled to another country
went to the Garden of God
to purge
the photographer, Rachael,
both of us in foreign lands
me, black,
her, white
prayed for me near the bridge
reminding me
I wasn't forgotten
by Him

The more
I meet
the more I know
it doesn't matter
the checkboxes
or class
or age
we all share
stories
moments
disappointments
hurt

joy
we all give up
and come back to life
in color

The Shack

He said he hated living in that shack
his wife made him buy
where he raised his children

so, when I visited
the Shack
I didn't notice it was broken
because his energy was so alive
we talked about reparations
and Mumia
and Washingtonian history
and the Post-Traumatic Slave Syndrome
and the Pearl Coalition

Then before lovemaking
we shared intimate details
of love lost
and Found
never Eternal
of struggles and betrayals
of loneliness

After lovemaking
we reminisced to old school
love jams like love was trying
to come in at that moment
to transform us
to something New
and Nice

and Warm

So, when he kissed
my body like we belonged
it agreed

And I wanted
to tell him everything
the trauma
the games
the lies I believed
and once told myself
the miles I ran
running after love
the steps I tracked
searching for myself

I challenged him to jump
off the boat
cross the river
come with me to the other side
so, we could be lovers
forget the past
forsake the games
mark one another as "soulmates"
I could get naked before him
with the lights on
unashamed
unclaimed by the pain
swallow his seeds whole
show him life

outside of himself
on another moon
to leave behind
what he wanted
for everything he needed
where he could finally
be a passenger

But he did not come
and when he did
never with both feet

Instead, he stayed
in the shack
that had been robbed
too many times
by neighbors who lost
their souls in a crap game
or to drugs a long time ago
when no one cared
about the crack epidemic

Reminding him of a past
he wanted to reclaim
a future left to recapture

And, I could hear his saxophone
drown it away
he said I was beautiful
called me Queen
without saying "My"

I knew
the spirit of the shack
had overtaken him
for a moment
drowned out the music
replaced a legacy
for a hard reality

That shack that meant promise
and family
beginnings
overthrown by swamp beasts
who visited the basement
possums that invaded his space
bullet shells lodged by the windows
teenagers who overlooked
the sacrifice of an already
worn Black man

I knew that he couldn't commit
to me
the way he had to the shack
it had a history I couldn't compete with
I was only to enjoy the times
watching
him
fix what was broken
replace what was old
repair the parts
while he was left searching

yearning for his due
His time
His place

The Leaving

I am happy to have left America
under a false democracy
where Our bodies bleed with no justice
or peace
and the evil have crippled
my people, many people
a system that crushes hope

I am happy to have left a home
broken when he left
with pieces scattered
across state lines
when we said we would start over
but soon discovered starting over
was too hard
commitment was only my part to play
I was left to do it by myself

I was happy to leave the noise of the TV
the ringing phone
that I was too distracted to notice
too numb to be fully present

So I could remember to listen to God
in Everything
look for God
Everywhere
never stop waiting for His answers

I was happy to be among people
who appreciated me
loved my hue and hair
asking me difficult, yet simple questions
Listening to other people's stories
remembering I am loved
realizing life is still worth this journey
whatever it may be
wherever it may go
I was happy
I left my body behind me
So, I could rediscover my soul
I didn't have to make the same mistakes
anymore
or repeat history's twisted tales
accepting them as the truth
because I was no longer afraid
my life was to be lived

regardless of self

Leaving home became the best of things
that's ever happened to me
now that I know what I know
the leaving has set me free

Feelings

I know you are trying
to hold on to your freedom
but you have to deal
with my feelings
now that you've made me able to feel

God knows my freedom means
everything to me
since I haven't been free for too long
I would hate to steal a piece of yours
but when I'm with you
I feel my heart pulling towards
you
even though I try to tuck it in
lock it up with a key
I can't deny how you make me feel
I don't want to love you
or fall in any kind of way
because I need to keep control
but...

You got me all up in my feelings

I feel myself thinking of you
in the classroom
at church
in my bedroom when I only want
to hear my ceiling fan
your face appears
laughing at me
for allowing you to come in
permeate me
seeping into my pores

Then I see us
wrapped up in each other
Horizontally
my legs in between yours
your arms gripping me
as my spirit leaves my body
to watch us sleep
and ask, "How did you get here?
how did I let you
sneak through the back door
taking a short cut through wooded roads
you navigated like a pro?"

Lately, I've found myself
trying to hide from you
but my feelings
won't let me run
anywhere but closer
I am revealing myself
I am not afraid to bleed
or let you see the scars
on my abdomen or breasts
because I know you'll kiss them
I am fighting with the love
I've always wanted
and the space I need to breathe

I know how this story plays out
I felt the way you "MARKED" me
For forever or right now
either way, it's nauseating
when your eyes catch mine
I wonder if you
can smell my fear
I tiptoe to the bathroom
away from your gaze
get on my knees

to pray
God won't let
these feelings overtake me
lose my way
or get stuck in between
your life and mine

These feelings creep in
at midnight
when the clock strikes
its perfect love language
The way you walk
or rant about some heroic community deed
or questions that need answers
I have lots of questions for you
about the way you intend to handle me
my mind
that wanders off to other places
while you're talking
I say, "Forget the answers
They're some things that are never meant
to be known"
Like this force I feel
when we are together

I want to make moments with you
all over the world
to bottle up these feelings
leave them on our stained sheets
hoping they will go away
or never leave

Cross the bridge

My man friend said
not to take that Black man serious
'cause those Washingtonians
don't cross the bridge
they don't take leaps
too deep
they don't look up at us
progressive, sensitive, spiritual
Black women
because they are too busy looking
at the souls on their shoes

He warned me not to make
the effort to cross the bridge
to spend time or money or love
I'd only be swallowed
by the politics because the men
become reflections of politicians
who smile and make promises
then eat you alive
I told him I would swim
if I had to cross that river

to get to him

Besides, I am from New York

where there are many rivers

that run wide and long

and deep

my love had the strength of those rivers

able to survive any tsunami

He laughed at my wits

said again, "some rivers

will let you drown in them

then spit you back out"

bridges were only

meant to be crossed when

there's some place to go

Washington will let you

into the city to wow you with

its monuments and tall handsome structures

that marked legacies

and histories and moments

you'll get lost in its circles

you won't be able to tell

who is authentic

who are invaders

the rats will eventually come out

even in the daylight

But I was from New York
use to the rats and the filthy
people who smelled bad
but told the best stories

I was used to the migrants
with different accents
complexions and ways
who made New York the best
place to live with their culture and food
while having an opinion
voice about it all
I was used to one borough being
apprehensive to go into another
unsure of the diversity of each
comfortable in one's own space
own place
where they belonged
where we crossed dirty rivers
by way of Underground trains
when we were unconscious of them
until we found ourselves

at our chosen place
and could see the landscapes
or looking out our windows
on bridges with high arches
worlds of promise bearing
the names of a borough we claimed

I was used to being able to spot a con
from miles away
them becoming my entertainment
for the evening

I was used to the musicians
who could make you fall in love
with their gift
sing a woman's panties off her
without getting to know each other's
last name because it was New York
where we were resilient, strong,
powerful like the waters, wars
walls of the city

And we, him and I, stood still
in one place

in Washington, DC
where I lost New York
let him test the quality
become the keeper of my rivers
but never actually cross the bridge

The
Awakening

I have always been

I have always been
hiding
rebelling
running away
from things too real
so I wouldn't have to really live
unmasked without question
withdrawn from fantasy
facing the truth
not the one I had made up
in my mind

Majority of my life
I have been
chasing unworthy potential
catching falling stars
long past their twinkle
mining dirty diamonds
with blood on their hands
and mindless intentions

I have been

fighting my future
my destiny
my calling
afraid of the best in me
belonged to another
when everything was all in me

Kelly and me

I couldn't help to think about Kelly
when I realized that my "sistah" friend
who preached love, light, forgiveness
blackness -all in one
was everything
but her Word

We went to see Kelly
at the Logan's Steakhouse
where she'd always greet us
with a smile
remember our order

In the beginning
it was our favorite spot
close to our jobs
far away from the noise
drama
Kelly was pleasant

We always talked a lot
my sistah and me

as I was limping along life
trying to find comfort
in a luncheon
or a date
or a night
that didn't remind me
my life was about to start again

Publicly, I laughed loud
cried hard when no one
was looking
about the pieces that had become
broken pieces
lost in the dirt
swept away by the wind

I pretended I wasn't two steps
from running into a hole
my sistah girl was just fine
I admired what seemed like security,
encouragement, commitment
friendship that lasted the test of time
Blackness that didn't rub off

Quietly, I went home
three steps to throwing my life
away or jumping off something high
to see if I could fly

Most times, the pressure became
so tight my pipes began to bursts
land on people unintentionally
because they didn't know or didn't care
I was just trying to walk on
take one more step
just one more step

Then I started to repair myself
recognize my part
want to clean up my act
be a part of the world again

And there she was
Kelly....
still walking, smiling
except had lost something
I listened as she told me
how her husband of over a decade

was caught in an affair
never came back

I went home and prayed for Kelly
cried for her
for the way the world would disappear
to her in the weeks and months ahead
She
the white waitress at Logan's
with blonde hair
And, I,
black college professor
with kinky black
had become one

Knowing a pain
that defies all life
race and culture
to kick you right in the gut
scratch you in the eyes
knock out your teeth
have you screaming toothless

We knew what it meant

to be around people all day
wearing the mask
faking the smile
stepping into a darkness
that has no end date or expiration

While I was halfway to my healing
rediscovering my smile
not afraid of selfies anymore
I knew that everyone would offer Kelly
condolences
then leave to their own worlds

In the meantime
I wrestled with my decision
to love again until love won
I fought my faith to trust God
then man
relented to listen to the God
who lived inside of me

I heard myself laugh again
hearty from deep in my belly
the moments began to clear

with precision and purpose

I took deep breaths
not sure if I wanted to see Kelly
be reminded of a past so grim
I had just returned from a solo trip to Europe
shaken off the last of my tears
made final decisions
was okay with eating at Logan's alone

Kelly came over smiling
like the smile had reached her belly
telling me the story of her divorce
and travels
free from love's requirements
the lakehouse in Georgia
now all hers
she finally found a room of her own
and I knew my prayers were answered

While I was grieving the loss of my sistah
who shared my hue
who deceived our friendship
I was experiencing the joy that came in knowing

Kelly and I were survivors
we were unbreakable now
our stories were not written in vain
or being read over our caskets
we had danced with devils
slept with the enemy
and Escaped
to rediscover life again
Kelly and me

White Man's World

In my years as a Black woman
I have been really mad at some white men
not because of their skin color
too few have taken me under his wing
taught me how to live in his world
or mine

At my last job I admired
A few
for their brilliance and demeanor
but they never seemed to be like me
I wasn't passive or country enough
I was rough like the streets of New York
but refined enough to be included
intellectual enough for the rhetoric
I tried going to lunch with them
sharing similar or familiar ideas
learn from them

Then a young white man joined the department
they rushed in to save what didn't need to be saved
brought him home to the family

that already belonged to him
introduce him to jokes that I was not privy to
I became angry again
envious

I wanted to tell them
I changed my hair
Because it showed the beauty of my culture
I wanted to show them that most of us can't talk about
summer vacations or homes
we are trying to maintain the homes we have
or plan to have
some of us have PTSD
even at work
from all the Black men and women murdered
dying
senseless deaths
And that due process
just meant sentencing without process or protection
America or its flag
means oppression
even those of us served
this country
some of us that still do

in the classroom, locker room, police station, boardroom

I want to tell them that I know that even now
in my position
and place
blessed
I must tread lightly
I am not afforded the same mistakes
or opportunities
or freedoms
give the history of inequality
that carried forth for generations
so they could have empathy for my people
not just accepting the elite
the brilliance
the talents
but our brokenness

And, in return, I wanted to share their privilege
Like Paul Tudor Jones who came once week to Bed-Stuy
to educate us
then gave us our first jobs as teenagers
yes, I wanted them to invite us into their homes and
families

offer us a seat at their table

teach us other languages

have honest dialogue

cook for us

then serve us a good meal

to reshape the minds

last a lifetime

Queen

He came to me
Asked if I could be his Queen
And, I was comfortable with that
because I know how he treats
the women in his life
even before he gave me this title

I remember how queens were treated
bartered, traded, and murdered
how their desires and needs were suppressed
for the wishes of kings
if he desired her at all
how she was used
as the object of stability for nations
a treasured tool
that did not have to be treasured
a commodity to cultures
always under watchful eye and scrutiny
liable to the will
favor of the people
serving, with attentiveness
assertion and grace

I wonder if she was allowed
to keep secrets or write her thoughts
enjoy her own gardens
alone

I know that she had desires that went unnoticed
like wearing pants to Sunday service
or her own court
or loving her own kind
like the Kings often did
indulging in her own lust

Or taking simple pleasure
in being unladylike
impolite
ungraceful
allowed to Be
unapologetically
disheveled

If she laughed out loud
or spit
or cursed her husband out

refused to bow

or show reverence in a crowd

when she felt the need

or interrupted an intellectual conversation

of men to call them out

on their Bullshit

especially, about the loves and needs

of a woman or roles of society

classes of people

or any of the lies or myths

many men make up

to prove they know it all

then lose his knowledge

over the pile of shit he created

I can't forget the queens

who were publicly beheaded

because of their defiance

or willful independence

replaced by younger, more prettier

more submissive

alternatives

Today, there are many

Queens

hiding behind their titles
afraid to claim their rightful throne
afraid to be alone
entertaining the masses
afraid to scream
acknowledge the pain that comes
with the position or step down
to be free of a heavy crown
because they'd rather their names
be etched on buildings and street signs
then on the legacy of their lives
that were lived
adorned by the masks
that seeped into their skin
become the permanent makeup
to their makeup

I turn to my lover
determined not to let my power fade
in moments
or arms
proud that he is by my side
all the sides of me
I am not afraid to expose

from time to time

say, "I want to be your Queen.

I want to be part of you

I want to be cloaked in the history of warriors

who were treated like Spartan women

who saved men

and nations

without sacrificing their freedom

or lives."

Nevertheless

Until I realize what makes us so powerful
Us, always moving,
periodically stopping to create love
along the way
make life more than what it seems to be
thankless
unrewarding to the righteous few

But, in you,
these days
I am reminded of the things
that count
family
nature
long walks
history
love
love-making
anywhere with you
stories that torment our souls
but we smile anyway
cause they make us

stronger
nevertheless

Sugar ain't as sweet
as honey
innocence is
and not knowing
what will come next
I'm scared
of what will come out of me
when there's no place
to go
when your walls break
and you can be vulnerable
when you stare at me
trust me with your tears
and fears
and say, "Chalet....

Nevertheless,
I am walking
not running
even when I want to
because I can feel

your resistance
I bump into you
unable to move you
to marry me
or not
merge scents
or create our own
fragrance

You inspire me
your drive
when life exhausts
your motivation
persistence
acceptance of me
I am on this journey
to figure out what is
flat or round
eternal or temporary
real or a façade

I am wrapping myself
in you
regardless of return

hiding in your chest hairs
running my hands
through your beard
listening to the staccato of your breaths
pace of steps
melody in your
unplayed sax

When it matters the most
we join together
risk losing our power
not our purpose
prepared for the outcome
either way
just in case
nevertheless

Kisses

Kisses are meant to be digested
swallowed whole
tasted
like fine wine
an indication of true love
rare like black opals
that stare into souls
endless like waterfalls

equivalent to rivers that flow
from a place that brings both joy and pain
but deeper
because of where it's located
not below the belt
but above the nipples
that provide nourishment
below the senses that bring discernment

Kisses are meant to be salivated
held onto
like precious memories
or metals

that don't fade with time
can never be taken away from the mind
lost in the mysteries of the Bermuda Triangle
never replicated
or replaced
only remembered
cherished

Strong like bamboo bridges
walked on by many men
fierce like hurricane winds
that bend palm trees
never break
collector of stories
of inevitable heartbreak
undeniable passion
ancient and traditional
like indigenous people
preserving their mother tongue
culture

Kisses are meant to be committed to
like the last piano note in a song
the source of connection

interconnectedness

of being one

with one another

the sharing and swapping of DNA

to indicate the need for belonging

owning someone other than yourself

revered

relished in

regarded as

possession of one's heart

One Breathe

What is this emotion?
This thing that makes one speak
what one does not feel
and if so, maybe unequal
at what level
what depth
what complexity

What is this thing?
That one might confess
what has not yet learned or taught
bears no degrees of competency
no tests of truth
other that one's deeds

What is this action?
That makes one give him/herself
so easily after being committed
this glorified feeling
this glorified living
that makes one feel
so replaceable

so temporary
so right in the midst of wrong

What is this thing?
that can so easily be mistaken
with so many faces
in so many places
can be a chameleon
or transform into
bitterness or hate
or fall out of
altogether
as if it never was

What is this thing?
We call love
with our twisted lies
deferred hope
deflated dreams

When love is BIG
HONEST
FORGIVING
WHOLE

FOREVER
All in ONE BREATHE

My Colorful Vagina

My vagina has color
but this color does
not afford privilege
because in some countries
they cut my clit
not as mutilation
but as a tradition
because my vagina is not
meant to bring pleasure
at least, not to myself
to not do so would risk
a future with a man
and the closer I am borne
by the water the more I am
expected to give back to the earth
my vagina affords me the right
to bear to bear and bear your children
and whatever else
the vagina can produce
in a reasonable enough time
before it becomes old
you're not interested

My vagina has color
But sometimes my seeds don't produce the flowers
you want
doesn't grow fast enough
with enough diversity
it gets choked by weeds
or fear
because of the pain
inflicted by loss
degradation
abandonment
even though, everyone knows
roses have thorns that cut
into the covering made by God
found to be unsacred
by ungrateful partakers

My vagina has color
but this color doesn't
differentiate experiences
because if you come close enough
yours smells just as funky as mine
On a hot summer day, when the wind fails to blow

And your scent is just as sweet as mine
When it's cherished and refreshed

My vagina has color
you ain't got no reason to judge
what color I may bring to the lives of others
if I choose
or the colors I choose to keep all to myself
for my pleasure
for my peace

Me Too

So many me toos
came out of the dark
So many me toos
still hiding
in the closet
beside the little girls
who pictured protection
in their daddies
or never knew protection at all
So many me toos
underneath the shadows
living in the reality
of the moments
that don't wash away with soap
or cover up with makeup
or go away with years

I celebrated all the me toos
in silence
I looked at the coward
who was me
I wanted to set up a booth

in the middle of Brooklyn
with a microphone
so everyone could tell
their me too stories out loud

Then I was searching for my soul
on a Sunday
when he appeared...
my childhood Pastor
who knew that his head security guard
sexually abused and tortured me
when I was 14
and naïve
and thought all "men of God"
knew love
then I lost my spirit
in the moment

I remembered sitting before him
broken
crying
lost
as I shared with him the story
I was afraid to share

for the sake of my mom
who was one of his first members
adoring fans
he prayed
when his faithful servant
admitted his deeds
then the pastor took me to his lawyer
Mr. Mickey
said that if I ever went public with my story
he would not testify on my behalf
and who would believe
when I was in the middle of searching
for love in all the wrong places
I understood silence
was golden, was mine

As the years went on
I talked too much
too soon
too loud
about everything except
my Me Toos

Today, in 2018,

I watched the creator
of Sunday Soul
On the Golden Globe
I felt empowered by a voice
I heard within
a voice revived
by all the other me toos
who were fearless
among powerful men

I pondered on men
who were not powerful
to anyone but the women
whose souls they stole
or childhood they ruined
or joy they corrupted

I knew that silence
That Golden silence
could be deadly
kill one within
murder the little girl
or the woman
wanting to come out

and scream

"Me Too"

Dear Lover,

Haven't we spent enough years
stuck in between promise and shit
Hurt and potential
I know you live your life in Top Secret mode
protecting what could be broken
guarding what could be taken
leaving behind and starting over
exhausted

I don't care about the color of your eyes
if they don't turn green for me
you can become my Incredible Hulk
And, I, your Wonder Woman
I can feel the passion you have for me
you can wonder if my love could get any better
I promise to arch my back in the ecstasy
when you finally reach the moment when you
could let it all go
and scream my name

I want the days without me to eat
you inside out

yearning for a desire not yet achieved

when you see me, you can't wait to taste

go places too deep for others to reach

we don't have to wait until that perfect moment

because no one will ever come

we will be stuck in moments that don't move

but pass us by

I want to make love in the truck

because you can't wait for the bedroom floor

or get married in Vegas on a whim

or travel to Europe with no destination in mind

or grab me when I come through the door

because the essence of my body scent

permeated the hallways

that penetrate your skin

because

life is too short

true love so rare

the pieces won't cover the holes

so, I will only accept the whole of you

because those walls only wear graffiti

that mark the pain of the past

stories never seep through

to the other side

moments that die in cement

No lover,
our stories will not go down
as those who gave away ourselves
to the hopeless perpetrators who lost their
conscious with our love
made us victims
of their twisted lies and empty souls

We will rise above the ashes
and love harder

Because

Because he loves history and culture
Because he's a Gemini and we click
Because a walk in the park with him is that and much
more
Because we love food
Because we can eat off each other's plate
Because when I'm bitchy he's the opposite
Because I can let my hair down
or cut it all off
or add to it
and be myself
Because he respects my space
Because he knows who he is
Because we can backpack in the woods
or explore the worlds together
Because we need no TVs or entertainment
Because our lives are so rich
we can tell stories
Because I can say he's fine and he can say she's fine
and no one is offended
Because he loves my blackness and I love his
Because my scars aren't ugly to him

and he wants the natural me

Because when we make love

we are actually making love

Because we've survived love lost

Because he gets me

Because there are never boring conversations

Because church doesn't define his spirituality

and neither does his past

Because he reads

and reads me

Because he's romantic

Because his family prays together

Because he loves his children

so he'll love mine

Because I see tomorrow in him

the future

Because I respect the man in him

And, he, the queen in me

Because he makes me want to listen more

Because I can trust him with my secrets

Because he's city and country all wrapped in one

Because I see God in him

Generations

Sitting in the hotel breakfast room
Black woman, approaching 40
creasing a new direction in life
behind a group of elderly Black women
Hehe-ing about what they've accomplished

The girl across seems to be approaching 30
we are both sitting alone
engrossed in the technology of our lives
for a second, we glance at each other, smile
acknowledging the mutual struggle
Black women, intelligent, alone
unpacking our lives in a room with no walls
or rules
or roles

One couldn't help but overhear
the cackling of our elders
about how the generations have changed
the young people "ain't got no respect"
the young black men "don't want us no more
don't want to marry us when they do"

how "chivalry is dead in this day and age"
or "how we don't dress right or cook
no meals anymore"
"cause we forgot how to be wives"
about Black young women "so concerned with
their career
not their men or children"
how black youth has made "technology their god
And, ohhh my, that music and clothes they wear are
detestable"
Then we look at each other again
this time with no smile
saddened by the promise and hope
our elders express
in today's black women
that belong to a generation
when black boys live off the success
drive of powerful black women
who have forgotten their worth
because of loneliness and desperation
because, like the boys, something
inside them has died
black men look for beauty standards in Europeans
and the black woman is left empty

by the "Real Housewives"
who were once hoes and mistresses
that left a family broken
as "our" men move on to the next best thing
whatever color that may be
black women are left fighting for child support and
spousal right but
most importantly, our dignity that ran away
because building the black man we loved...
broke us

Suffering in silent depression
to uphold the title of "Strong Black Women"
that, some days, we want to throw away
when we are exposed as the weakest link
we can find a place to hide
behind our degrees and beautiful children
encouraging words from a real sistah or brotha
or fake sisterhoods
reminding us that we must always be one step ahead
one outfit better
we refuse to shed a tear
we forsake our psychologists' bills that do not
always heal the pain

only allow us to cope

Where we are the most educated
but still grossly underpaid
underrepresented
undervalued
even among our own

I am thinking of my sistah
friend Sonia Sanchez
Or my aunts Karen Gustus
Priscilla Storey
Or women like Karen Sweeting, Patricia Gary, Shewanda
Riley and Martha Glenn
or natural mentors of another race
but pure hearts like Alice Oshins
Linda Mann or mothers like
Malissa Redmond and mine
who would have offered an encouraging word or two
regardless of what they thought to be broken
or full of dysfunction
who have given us a seat at their table
to share a wisdom or two
allow a tear to fall with gentle reproach, if needed

who would have dropped a seed
of knowledge or experience or love
or offered a prayer
for a stranger they barely knew

Because they understand
one moment can change a life
one word can change a mine
all generations need to lean
on one another
to gleam from what one has to give
or receive
without judgment
or Cause
or payment for services rendered
that all generations depend on another
for our legacies to be carried on
continued
for the future generations to thrive

ReLive

When you come
so close to death
You can forget how to live

You can get so used to pain
you have no desire for true love

You can give so much away
being empty feels normal

But, you must know that life is made
to RELIVE again
and death comes so something
can be reborn

Spirits can become so stale
hearts so cold
piercings are no longer felt
words no longer bear meaning
bonds lose all their ties, so much so
your lies become the truth

Daily living can be so much of a game
players bear no resemblance
to anything human
the pieces all fade
while the world stands still
where you feel like your pain
the only thing real

Your senses can become so dull
that the flowers seem painted
the smiles stale
touches fragmented

You begin to bet on death's timing
call for destinies
that are destined to last
only for a moment

Because you forgot
life is made to live again
even in death
everything and everyone can be reborn

Femininity can transform into masculinity

true gentlemen can become callous creatures
after one deep wound
blood can become thinner than water
although the bruises are old
and broken bones can come back to haunt you
in the middle of your prime

You don't know how to turn back the clock
to begin again
by rediscovering life, all can be reborn
even in death, new life can be found
celebrated
even in loss and heartbreak, one can choose to
RELIVE